HOLIDAYS AND FESTIVALS

Hanukkah

Nancy Dickmann

www.raintreepublishers.co.uk
Visit our website to find out
more information about
Raintree books.

To order:
☎ Phone 0845 6044371
🖶 Fax +44 (0) 1865 312263
🖥 Email myorders@raintreepublishers.co.uk

Customers from outside the UK please telephone +44 1865 312262

Raintree is an imprint of Capstone Global Library Limited, a company incorporated in England and Wales having its registered office at 7 Pilgrim Street, London, EC4V 6LB – Registered company number: 6695582

Edited by Sian Smith, Nancy Dickmann, and Rebecca Rissman
Designed by Steve Mead
Picture research by Elizabeth Alexander
Production by Victoria Fitzgerald
Originated by Capstone Global Library Ltd
Printed and bound in China by South China Printing Company Ltd

ISBN 978 0 431 00723 6
14 13 12 11 10
10 9 8 7 6 5 4 3 2 1

British Library Cataloguing in Publication Data
Dickmann, Nancy.
  Hanukkah. -- (Holidays and festivals)
  1. Hanukkah--Pictorial works--Juvenile literature.
  I. Title II. Series
  394.2'67-dc22

Acknowledgements
We would like to thank the following for permission to reproduce photographs: Alamy pp. **4**, **9** (© Israel images), **7** (© Design Pics Inc.), **10** (© UpperCut Images), **13** (© Art Directors & TRIP); Corbis pp. **5** (© Roy Morsch), **16** (© Leland Bobbé), **19** (© Owen Franken); Getty Images pp. **12** (Sean Gallup), **14** (Gali Tibbon/AFP), **17** (James And James), **20** (Jonathan Nackstrand/AFP), **21**, **23 top** (Stephen Chernin); iStockphoto pp. **22 left** (© Sandra O'Claire), **23 bottom** (© Rafael Ramirez Lee); Photolibrary p. **6** (The Print Collector/Imagestate); Shutterstock pp. **11**, **23 middle** (© Noam Armonn), **15** (© Lisa F. Young), **18** (© Tata), **22 middle** (© Elzbieta Sekowska), **22 right** (© Jeff Banke); The Bridgeman Art Library p. **8** (© British Library Board. All Rights Reserved).

Front cover photograph of family lighting Menorah reproduced with permission of Corbis (© Roy Morsch). Back cover photograph reproduced with permission of Corbis (© Roy Morsch).

We would like to thank Diana Bentley, Dee Reid, Nancy Harris, and Richard Aubrey for their invaluable help in the preparation of this book.

Every effort has been made to contact copyright holders of material reproduced in this book. Any omissions will be rectified in subsequent printings if notice is given to the publishers.

Contents

What is a festival?. 4

The story of Hanukkah 6

Lighting candles. 10

Celebrating Hanukkah today. 14

Things to look for 22

Picture glossary 23

Index 24

What is a festival?

A festival is a time when people come together to celebrate.

Jewish people celebrate Hanukkah in the winter.

The story of Hanukkah

Long ago, the Jewish army won
a battle. They wanted to celebrate.

Their special lamp needed oil.

There was only enough oil to light it for one day. But the oil lasted for eight days.

8

Jewish people believe God made
this happen.

Lighting candles

Hanukkah lasts for eight nights.

menorah

People light candles in a menorah each night.

People say prayers each night.

The light reminds them of God's power.

Celebrating Hanukkah today

Hanukkah is a happy time.

It is called the Festival of Lights.

People give gifts or money.

People share food.

doughnut

People eat foods cooked in oil.

latkes

People eat potato pancakes
called latkes.

dreidel

People sing and play games.

Some people pray together in
the synagogue.

Things to look for

dreidel

latkes

menorah

Have you seen these things? They make people think of Hanukkah.

Picture glossary

 **Jewish people** people who follow the teachings of the religion Judaism

 **menorah** special candle holder used at Hanukkah. It has spaces for nine candles.

 **synagogue** building where Jewish people go to worship

Index

candles 10, 11

gifts 16

God 9, 13

menorah 11, 22

oil 7, 8, 18

prayers 12

Notes for parents and teachers

Before reading

Ask the children if they know what holidays and festivals are. Can they name any festivals they celebrate with their families? Can they think of any festivals where candles are used? Explain that Hanukkah is a festival celebrated by Jewish people, who follow the religion of Judaism. Hanukkah is called the Festival of Lights.

After reading

• Talk about the story of Hanukkah and ask the children why they think foods fried in oil are eaten at this festival. Show the children how to make a typical Hanukkah food such as potato pancakes (also called 'latkes').

• Explain that the menorah used during Hanukkah (also called a 'channukiah') is different from the one that burned in the story of Hanukkah. By comparing these in the book children can find out that the menorah in the story had seven branches and Hanukkah menorahs have nine. Eight of the candles in the Hanukkah menorah stand for the eight nights of Hanukkah and the ninth candle, called the 'shammas' or 'helper', is used to light the others. On each night of Hanukkah one more candle is lit, building up until the eighth night of the festival when all eight candles are lit.

• Try to find a wooden dreidel or make a dreidel template on paper. Explain the meanings of the four Hebrew letters on the dreidel, which stand for 'a great miracle happened there', translated into Hebrew. Teach the children to play the dreidel game.